Houghton Mifflin Harcourt

JOURNEYS

Close Reader

GRADE

3

Consumable

Printed in the U.S.A.

ISBN 978-0-544-86945-5

5 6 7 8 9 10 0877   23 22 21 20 19 18 17

4500682234   B C D E F G

UNIT 1
Good Citizens

UNIT 2
Look and Listen

UNIT 3
Lesson Learned

UNIT 4
Natural Wonders

UNIT 5
Going Places

Houghton
Mifflin
Harcourt

JOURNEYS

Close Reader

UNIT 1
Good Citizens

Background In a one-room schoolhouse, all the students learn together in one room. Long ago, these tiny schools were important in small towns with just a few families.

Setting a Purpose Read the text to learn about the history of one-room schoolhouses.

One-Room Schoolhouses

CLOSE READ
Notes

① Read As you read, look for text evidence.

- Circle the title of this selection.
- Underline a sentence that tells how students felt about going to a one-room schoolhouse.

One-room schoolhouses were once common in America. In the early 1900s, there were more than 250,000. Some children today still attend one-room schoolhouses.

Students of all ages were **proud** to learn in these small schools. There was usually one teacher and no principal.

proud:

2 **Read** As you read, look for text evidence.

- Circle the words that tell what this page is about.
- Underline a sentence that tells what students learned in one-room schoolhouses.

Daily Life

A ringing bell often announced the start of each day. Students did **chores**, such as bringing in wood for cooking and heating or raising a flag that soared in the sky above the schoolyard.

The teacher worked with one or two students at a time. They studied subjects such as reading, math, history, spelling, and handwriting. Students wrote on small slates, or blackboards, because paper was too expensive.

chores:

3 **Reread and Discuss** Reread the page. What activities did students do in one-room schoolhouses that most students don't do today? Cite text evidence in your discussion.

SHORT RESPONSE

Cite Text Evidence What does the heading tell you about the information in this section? Cite details from the text in your response.

_____

_____

_____

_____

4 **Read** As you read, look for text evidence.

- Circle the photo of Mary McLeod Bethune.
- Underline two sentences that explain why Mary McLeod Bethune is a famous American.

Famous Students

famous:

     Some **famous** Americans learned in one-room schoolhouses. Mary McLeod Bethune went to one in South Carolina in the late 1800s. She became one of America's great teachers. She fought for **civil rights**.

civil rights:

     Former United States President Lyndon Johnson attended a one-room schoolhouse in Texas. Johnson was born near Stonewall, Texas, in 1908. He was President from 1963 until 1969.

Mary McLeod Bethune

Lyndon Johnson

5 **Reread** Reread the page. What can you infer about the importance of one-room schoolhouses in American history? Cite text evidence in your response.

_____

_____

_____

6 **Read** As you read, look for text evidence.

- Circle the name of the person shown in the photograph.
- Underline a detail in the main text that tells more about this person.

Schoolhouses Today

mainland:

Some students still study in a one-room schoolhouse. In winter, fewer than one hundred people live on Monhegan Island, in Maine. It is too far to go to the **mainland** for classes, so students attend the island's little schoolhouse.

In most places, bigger schools opened when one-room schoolhouses became too small. People became worried about losing the fine old buildings. Some became museums. You can tour a school in South Dakota just like one that writer Laura Ingalls Wilder attended.

Other schoolhouses became stores, restaurants, and homes. These little buildings are certainly important pieces of American history.

Laura Ingalls Wilder, writer of *Little House on the Prairie*, strolled several miles to a one-room schoolhouse.

7 **Reread and Discuss** Reread the page. What does the heading explain about the text on this page? Cite text evidence in your discussion.

SHORT RESPONSE

Cite Text Evidence Why did some one-room schoolhouses become museums, stores, and restaurants? Cite text evidence in your response.

_____

_____

_____

Background A court is a government building. In a courtroom, a group of people called a jury decides whether someone broke a law. Juries are an important part of the court system in the United States.

Setting a Purpose Read the selection to learn what a jury does.

You Be the Jury

by Ruth Masters

① **Read** As you read, look for text evidence. Circle the title on this page.

citizens:

Citizens of the United States live in a country where they can take part in their government. Good citizens work together in many ways to serve their government.

② Read As you read, look for text evidence.

- Circle the heading. Then circle a sentence that tells what this section is mostly about.
- Underline two sentences that tell how people learn that it's their turn to serve on a jury.

Being Called to Duty

One way that citizens can help their state government is by serving on a jury. A jury is a group of people that decides whether someone is guilty of breaking a law or not guilty.

Members of the jury are called jurors. When people are **accused** of breaking laws, they have the right to have their case heard by juries. In return, citizens also have a **duty** to serve as a juror, if asked.

Citizens take turns serving jury duty. A letter tells a person that it is his or her turn. It tells when to go to court.

accused:

duty:

③ Reread and Discuss Reread the page. What rights and duties do citizens have in the United States? Cite text evidence in your discussion.

SHORT RESPONSE

Cite Text Evidence Why is serving on a jury an important duty for citizens? Cite text evidence in your response.

_____

_____

_____

4 **Read** As you read, look for text evidence.

- Circle a text feature that tells what the text on this page is mostly about.
- Underline the sentences that tell who is in a courtroom.

Sitting at Trial

At court, a juror sits in a room with other jury members. Other people in the courtroom are the judge, the defendant, and lawyers. The defendant is the person who is accused of breaking a law. A lawyer knows the laws. He or she speaks for the defendant. The lawyers tell the facts about what happened. They may put **witnesses** on the stand. Lawyers on each side try to convince the jury to vote in their favor.

witnesses:

lawyer   judge   witness

5 **Reread** Reread the page. What does a lawyer do to help a defendant? Cite text evidence in your response.

_____

_____

_____

6 **Read** As you read, look for text evidence.
Underline the sentences that tell what jury members must
do at the end of a trial.

Making a Decision

At the end, it is time for the jury to decide whether a
law was broken. Jury members must think about the
facts. They must listen to one another. Then they must
make a choice.

The jury's decision is called the verdict. The verdict of
guilty or not guilty is read out loud. The jury might say,
"We find the defendant guilty." After that, the trial is
over. The jurors did their duty.

jury   **lawyer**

7 **Reread and Discuss** Reread the page. What does the heading on this
page tell about the text? Cite text evidence in your discussion.

SHORT RESPONSE

Cite Text Evidence What did you learn about how juries make decisions?
Cite text evidence in your response.

_____

_____

_____

Background When people offer to help others, it's called volunteering, or doing service. Volunteers help in many different ways. They don't do this work for money. They do it to make the world a better place.

Setting a Purpose Read the selection to learn about Global Youth Service Day.

Kids Making a Difference

by Jeremy Stone

CLOSE READ
Notes

① **Read** As you read, look for text evidence.

- Circle the title. Then circle the words that help explain what this section of the text is about.
- Underline a sentence that tells when Global Youth Service Day takes place.

A Day to Help

Would you like the chance to figure out fun ways to **improve** your school, block, or town? Put your ideas into action in April on Global Youth Service Day!

improve:

2 **Read** As you read, look for text evidence.

- Circle the words that tell about the photo.
- Underline a sentence that tells how some kids help people who can't afford food.

charities:

On this day, kids across the country work to make their communities safer and cleaner, or to help others. Some collect food for people who can't afford it. Others raise money for local **charities**. They earn this money by holding **fundraisers** or getting customers at local shops to make donations.

fundraisers:

Global Youth Service Day began in 1988. Celebration of this day is spreading around the world.

3 **Reread and Discuss** Reread the page. How do kids help local charities on Global Youth Service Day? Cite text evidence in your discussion.

SHORT RESPONSE

Cite Text Evidence How does the caption on this page help you understand the photo and the main text? Cite details from the text in your response.

_____

_____

_____

_____

④ **Read** As you read, look for text evidence.

- Circle the words that help explain what this section of the text is about.
- Circle the place on the map where kids pick up trash.

Texas Kids Help Out

On Global Youth Service Day in Arlington, Texas, more than 800 kids help their community. Some visit nursing homes. Others plant flowers. In **historic** Arlington Cemetery, youth baseball teams pick up trash. The cemetery is next to the teams' ball fields.

After a busy day, it's party time in Vandergriff Park! The hardworking kids gather there to celebrate.

historic:

⑤ **Reread** Reread the page and look back at the map. What can you learn from the small map of Texas inside the larger map?

_____

_____

6 **Read** As you read, look for text evidence.
Underline a sentence that tells what the murals in San Francisco are about.

Helping with Art

One group of artists in San Francisco is helping children make their city beautiful all year round. Adult artists from a group called Kids Serve go to schools around the city. The artists help students plan special **murals**. The murals are usually about topics the children are studying in class.

Once the mural is planned, the children work together to create the mural in a public area. When it is done, neighbors are contacted and invited to celebrate and enjoy the mural.

murals:

7 **Reread and Discuss** Reread the page. What does the heading explain about the text on this page? Cite text evidence in your discussion.

SHORT RESPONSE

Cite Text Evidence   Why do artists and children create murals in San Francisco? How is this activity similar to others you read about in the text? Cite text evidence in your response.

_____

_____

_____

_____

Background Workers build bridges so people can cross busy roads or bodies of water such as canals. Without bridges, it would be much harder to travel.

Setting a Purpose Read the text to learn about different kinds of bridges.

Bridges

by Matthew Danzeris

① Read As you read, look for text evidence. Circle the title of this text.

Bridges help people get from place to place. They join communities. They stretch across waterways and the swirling tide. They take us over roadways and landforms. People have been building bridges for thousands of years. They think about how long the bridge must be. They think about what the bridge will cost. Then they decide what kind of bridge to build.

(2) Read As you read, look for text evidence.

- Circle the words that tell what the two text sections on this page are about.
- Underline two sentences that tell benefits of beam bridges.

Arch Bridge

An arch bridge uses sturdy curved structures called arches. The arches rest on strong supports called **abutments**. Abutments are set firmly in the solid ground below the water.

abutments:

Beam Bridge

The beam bridge is the simplest kind of bridge for a crew to build. It costs the least, too!

piers:

A beam bridge has a beam. It lies across supports called **piers**. The piers must be close enough together to give the beam strength. That way, the roadway won't bend or sag too much when traffic crosses it. Each **span** of a beam bridge is usually less than 250 feet long.

span:

(3) Reread and Discuss Reread the page. What is the purpose of piers on a beam bridge? Cite text evidence in your discussion.

SHORT RESPONSE

Cite Text Evidence What useful information do the headings give you about the text sections on this page? What do the headings tell you about how the text is organized? Cite details from the text in your response.

_____

_____

_____

4 **Read** As you read, look for text evidence.

- Circle the words that label parts of the diagram.
- Underline a text clue that helps you understand the meaning of the word *suspension*.

suspension:

anchorage:

Suspension Bridge

A **suspension** bridge can stretch as far as 7,000 feet. That's more than a mile! On a suspension bridge, the roadway hangs from cables. The cables rest on top of towers. At each end of the bridge, an **anchorage** holds the cables in place.

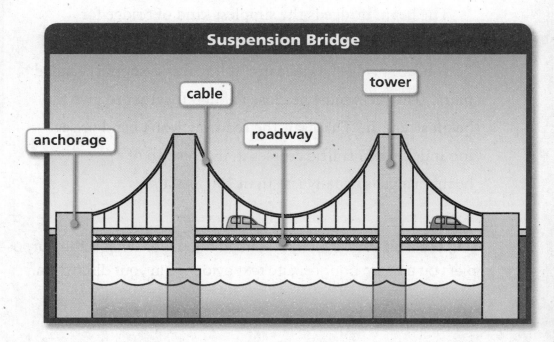

Suspension Bridge

anchorage   cable   roadway   tower

5 **Reread** Reread the page. How does the diagram help you understand the main text on this page? Cite text evidence in your response.

_____

_____

_____

6 **Read** As you read, look for text evidence.

- Circle the words that give information about this section of the text.
- Underline a sentence that tells how builders stay safe when they work on a bridge.

Building Bridges

A large crew of workers builds most bridges. The work is dangerous. Workers wear **harnesses** to stay safe when they are balancing up high. Strong winds and foggy weather make the work even more dangerous. Builders cling to the bridge. When at last the work is done, excitement grips everyone. A ceremony may be held to celebrate.

harnesses:

7 **Reread and Discuss** Reread the page. How is the heading on this page different from the headings on earlier pages? Cite text evidence in your discussion.

SHORT RESPONSE

Cite Text Evidence Why is bridge-building a dangerous job? Which type of bridge might be most dangerous to build? Cite text evidence from this page and the rest of the text in your response.

_____

_____

_____

_____

_____

Background In the United States, baseball is closely linked to warm weather. Professional baseball teams play between April and October each year, when the weather usually is warm (or at least not freezing cold!). School baseball teams play in the spring, and groups of neighborhood kids play all summer long.

Setting a Purpose Read the poem to learn how the poet feels about baseball and summer.

HOMER

by Nikki Grimes

① **Read** As you read, look for text evidence. Underline a sentence that explains why baseball is called "America's Pastime."

pastime:

What did most kids do for fun before television, computers, and video games were invented? They played baseball! For years it was the most widely played sport in the United States. That's how baseball came to be called "America's **Pastime**."

② **Read** As you read, look for text evidence.
Underline two sentences from the poem that use
figurative language.

HOMER

Summer words, like *raspberry ice,*
beach, and *barbecue,* are all gone now.
But I find another warm word,
shaped like a bat. HOMER.
I wrap my fingers tightly round it
and swing.

homer:

SHORT RESPONSE

Cite Text Evidence To what does the poet compare the word *homer*? Why does
she call *homer* a warm word? Cite details from the text in your response.

_____

_____

_____

_____

_____

UNIT 2
Look and Listen

Background Bats are small flying mammals that usually are active at night and sleep during the day. The looping, soaring mother bat in this poem is hunting for insects in the night air.

Setting a Purpose Read the poem to experience a night in the life of a newborn bat and his mother.

A Bat Is Born

by Randall Jarrell   illustrated by Sue Todd

(1) Read As you read, look for text evidence.

- Circle three words that describe the baby bat.
- Underline words that describe the way the mother bat flies.

doubling:

somersaulting:

A bat is born
Naked and blind and pale.
His mother makes a pocket of her tail
And catches him. He clings to her long fur
By his thumbs and toes and teeth.
And then the mother dances through the night
Doubling and looping, soaring, **somersaulting**—
Her baby hangs on underneath.

② Read As you read, look for text evidence.

- Circle the words that tell what the mother bat's "high, sharp cries" are similar to.
- Underline the words that tell why the mother bat cries out in the night.

All night, in happiness, she hunts and flies.

Her high sharp cries

Like shining needlepoints of sound

Go out into the night and, **echoing** back,

Tell her what they have touched.

She hears how far it is, how big it is,

Which way it's going;

She lives by hearing.

echoing:

③ Reread and Discuss Reread this part of the poem. How do the poet's words help you picture what is happening? Cite text evidence in your discussion.

SHORT RESPONSE

(Cite Text Evidence) Why does the poet say the mother bat "lives by hearing"? Cite details from the text in your response.

_____

_____

_____

_____

4 Read As you read, look for text evidence.

- Circle the words that rhyme in this part of the poem. (Hint: They are not all at the ends of the lines!)
- Underline words that give readers an image of how close the mother is to her baby.

The mother eats the moths and gnats she catches
In full flight; in full flight
The mother drinks the water of the pond
She skims across. Her baby hangs on tight.
Her baby drinks the milk she makes him
In moonlight or starlight, in mid-air.
Their single shadow, printed on the moon
Or fluttering across the stars,
Whirls on all night; at daybreak
The tired mother flaps home to her **rafter**.

rafter:

5 Reread Reread this part of the poem. Why is the mother bat tired when she flaps home? What words and phrases from the poem help you know this? Cite text evidence in your response.

_____

_____

_____

_____

6 **Read** As you read, look for text evidence.
Underline the text that describes how the bats sleep.

The others all are there.

They hang themselves up by their toes,

They wrap themselves in their brown wings.

Bunched upside down, they sleep in air.

Their sharp ears, their sharp teeth, their
    quick sharp faces

Are dull and slow and **mild**.

All the bright day, as the mother sleeps,

She folds her wings about her sleeping child.

mild:

7 **Reread and Discuss** Reread this part of the poem. In what way does the mother bat stay the same, even when she is sleeping? Cite text evidence in your discussion.

SHORT RESPONSE

Cite Text Evidence What language does the poet use to show how the bats change from night to day? Cite text evidence in your response.

_____

_____

_____

_____

Jack Draws a Beanstalk

by Anne O'Brien

① **Read** As you read, look for text evidence. Underline words in the text that give you hints that this story will be make-believe.

sketched:

Jack loved to make up stories and illustrate them. He did research to find out what things looked like. He **sketched** his ideas over and over on tracing paper. He colored the pictures with different textures. When his pictures were just right, he could imagine that his stories were real.

One night, Jack drew a bean vine. "I wish I had a magic bean vine, just like in the fairy tale," Jack said. He worked on the sketches until he fell asleep.

② **Read** As you read, look for text evidence.

- Circle a sentence that tells about two different actions: one that could happen in real life, and one that could not.
- Underline text that hints that Jack may be in danger.

When he woke up, there was the bean vine, growing out of his sketchbook. His **scribbles** were coming to life!

Jack grabbed his sketchbook and pencil and began to climb the beanstalk. He came to a huge castle in the clouds, just like the one in the fairy tale. And there was the giant's wife, who happily served Jack tea.

"But you must leave before my husband comes home," the giant's wife said. "He might try to eat you for dinner!"

scribbles:

③ **Reread and Discuss** Reread the page. What is the first thing that happens that could happen only in a make-believe story? Cite text evidence in your discussion.

SHORT RESPONSE

Cite Text Evidence How does Jack act differently from someone in a realistic story? Cite details from the text and the illustration in your response.

_____

_____

_____

_____

4 **Read** As you read, look for text evidence.

- Circle a sentence that compares the giant's sounds to something in nature.
- Underline a sentence that shows Jack is finally scared.

rumble:

Just then they heard a **rumble** like loud thunder.

"He's home early!" cried the wife. She popped Jack into her apron pocket.

Jack heard the giant's voice yelling, "FEE FI FO FUM!"

"Oh, no," Jack said to himself. "This is too much like the fairy tale! The only tools I've got to help me escape are my sketchbook and pencil!"

Jack was shaking when he began to draw. He drew a magic hen. The hen came to life and laid a golden egg, just like in the fairy tale.

"Cluck, cluck!"

5 **Reread** Reread the page. How will Jack get OUT of trouble the same way he got INTO trouble? Cite text evidence in your response.

_____

_____

_____

© Houghton Mifflin Harcourt Publishing Company

6 **Read** As you read, look for text evidence.

- Circle two sentences about events that could not happen in real life.
- Underline a sentence about an event that could happen in real life.

The wife reached into her pocket and pulled out the hen and the golden egg. While the two giants **exclaimed** over the hen, Jack escaped out of the castle and climbed down the vine.

When Jack got home, he opened his sketchbook. He erased the bean vine as fast as he could. "From now on, I'll be careful about what I wish for!" said Jack.

exclaimed:

7 **Reread and Discuss** Reread the page. How do the hen and the golden egg make it possible for Jack to escape? Cite text evidence in your discussion.

SHORT RESPONSE

Cite Text Evidence What is the lesson of this fairy tale? Is this a lesson readers can use in real life? Why or why not? Cite text evidence in your response.

_____

_____

_____

_____

_____

Background Folktales are stories that have been told for a long time. They often include a moral, or lesson. This folktale is hundreds of years old and has been told in many countries. Each country tells the story a bit differently.

Setting a Purpose Read the text to learn what happens when a man goes in search of a treasure.

The Old Man and His Dream

CLOSE READ Notes

1 **Read** As you read, look for text evidence.
- Circle the two characters named on this page.
- Underline the sentence that tells about the characters' problem.

An old man and his wife lived in a small village. The couple had come upon hard times, and they were very poor. Often the old man lay awake all night, worrying about the future.

After many nights of tossing and turning, the old man was **exhausted**. One afternoon, after eating a lunch of watery soup, he lay down for a nap. He fell instantly into a deep sleep.

exhausted:

30

© Houghton Mifflin Harcourt Publishing Company • Image Credits: ©photoneye/iStock/Getty Images

2 **Read** As you read, look for text evidence.

- Circle the words that tell what the man learns in his dream.
- Underline what the man says to his wife after his dream.

As he slept, the old man had a strange dream. In it, a voice told him to travel over hills and through valleys to a far-off city. There he would uncover a great treasure in a house with a bright blue door.

The old man woke from his nap and jumped to his feet. He grabbed his hat and coat. Then he called to his wife, who was **tending** the yellow rose bush in their garden. "Goodbye, my dear! When I return, our troubles will be over!"

tending:

3 **Reread and Discuss** Reread the page. What does the old man do as soon as he wakes up? What does this tell you about him? Cite text evidence in your discussion.

SHORT RESPONSE

Cite Text Evidence Why do you think the man tells his wife, "When I return, our troubles will be over"? Cite details from the text in your response.

_____

_____

_____

_____

(4) **Read** As you read, look for text evidence.

- Circle the words that tell where the man goes when he reaches the city.
- Underline words that tell the woman's opinion about whether dreams are real.

wandered:

enormous:

The old man rushed off. He walked over hills and valleys to the city that lay beyond. He **wandered** down many narrow, winding streets, until finally he reached a house with a bright blue door, just like the one he'd heard of in his dreams.

When the old man knocked on the door, it swung open. A woman stood before him. She asked, "What can I do for you, sir?" The old man was speechless for a moment. But then he spilled out the story of his dream and the treasure that awaited him.

The woman laughed and said, "Ah, it would be a fine thing if all our dreams came true!" She added sadly, "But only fools believe in dreams. Why, just last night I had a dream similar to yours. In it I walked over hills and valleys to a small village. I reached a stone cottage with a lovely rose garden. I dug beneath a yellow rose bush, and there was an **enormous** pile of gold coins!"

(5) **Reread** Reread the page. Why does the woman share her dream with the old man? Cite text evidence in your response.

_____

_____

_____

6 **Read** As you read, look for text evidence.

- Circle the text that gives clues about how the old man feels after he hears the woman's dream.

- Underline words that tell what the old man does when he gets home.

Suddenly, the old man grabbed the woman's hand and shook it **vigorously**. "Thank you, my dear woman!" he cried, and he rushed off. Over hills and valleys he raced, till he reached his own cottage. He ran to the garden and dug beneath the yellow rose bush. There he found an enormous pile of gold coins.

"The treasure was right here all along!" the old man said. "But I had to travel far to find it."

vigorously:

7 **Reread and Discuss** Reread the page. Why is the old man in such a rush to get home after he hears the woman's dream? Cite text evidence in your discussion.

SHORT RESPONSE

Cite Text Evidence What do you think is the moral, or lesson, of this story? Cite text evidence in your response.

_____

_____

_____

_____

Background Kamishibai (kah-mee-she-bye) means "paper theater." Kamishibai art is said to have started in Japan in the late 1920s. But telling stories with pictures started hundreds of years before that.

Setting a Purpose Read the text to learn the history of kamishibai artists in Japan.

The True Story of Kamishibai

by Elizabeth Manning

© Houghton Mifflin Harcourt Publishing Company • Image Credits: ©Kenneth Hamm/Photo Japan

CLOSE READ
Notes

①Read As you read, look for text evidence.

- Circle the title and the words that tell about this section of the text.
- Underline a sentence that tells how a kamishibai man let children know he had arrived.

rickety:

clacking:

Clacking Sticks

Long ago in Japan, kamishibai men rode around on bicycles with wooden boxes on the back. Each man parked his **rickety** bike in his own special part of town. At the sound of two wooden sticks **clacking** together, children came running. They bought the candy the man kept in a drawer in the wooden box. Then they waited.

② Read As you read, look for text evidence.

- Circle the words that tell about this section of the text.
- Underline a sentence that describes the kamishibai man's first step in telling a story.

Stories in the Street

    The kamishibai man put a picture card in the frame at the top of the box. He began to tell a familiar story. One by one, he slipped the pictures in and out. His movements were smooth, not **jerky**. In case his memory was blurry, parts of the story were on the back of each picture. The kamishibai storytellers always stopped at an exciting part. The children came back another day to hear what happened next. They greeted the end of the story with **applause**.

jerky:

applause:

③ Reread and Discuss Reread the page. What does the heading tell you about this section of the text? Cite text evidence in your discussion.

SHORT RESPONSE

(Cite Text Evidence) Why did the kamishibai man always stop his story at an exciting part? Cite details from the text in your response.

_____

_____

_____

_____

④ **Read** As you read, look for text evidence.

- Circle the words that tell about this section of the text.
- Underline a sentence that tells when kamishibai became less popular.

What Happened Next?

In the 1960s, something changed. Children stayed indoors after school, leaving the streets **vacant**. Paper pictures were no match for stories shown on a new invention called television. The noise of televisions blasted from homes. The sound of two wooden sticks clacking together was now a rude **interruption**. Were the days of kamishibai over?

vacant:

interruption:

⑤ **Reread** Reread the page. Why did children lose interest in kamishibai? Cite text evidence in your response.

_____

_____

_____

_____

6 **Read** As you read, look for text evidence.

- Circle the names of two new kinds of Japanese art.
- Underline a sentence that tells where kamishibai takes place today.

A New Chapter

Some kamishibai artists found work making other kinds of pictures. They drew for the new Japanese comics, called manga. Some of their comics were made into cartoon movies, called anime. Today people create and read manga and anime all over the world.

Children can still listen to the old paper-theater stories. Storytellers have brought kamishibai to schools and libraries in Japan and the United States. This paper theater doesn't arrive on the back of a bicycle, but the stories and pictures are still wonderful!

7 **Reread and Discuss** Reread the page. Why did kamishibai artists begin to make other kinds of pictures? Cite text evidence in your discussion.

SHORT RESPONSE

Cite Text Evidence How is kamishibai different today from the way it was long ago? How is it similar? Cite text evidence in your response.

_____

_____

_____

_____

_____

Background Scientist and inventor Thomas Edison created the kinetoscope, a device for watching moving pictures without sound. About 30 years later, the first "talkies," or movies with sound, began.

Setting a Purpose Read the text to learn about the development of movies.

Moving Pictures

by Andrew Patterson

CLOSE READ
Notes

① Read As you read, look for text evidence. Underline a sentence that names the invention that led to the development of movies.

conducted:

gadget:

You can thank the genius Thomas Edison every time you watch a movie. His laboratory **conducted** one moving picture experiment after another. Workers took just an occasional break. One invention of theirs led to the development of movies. That **gadget** was the kinetoscope.

The Kinetoscope

The kinetoscope was a wooden box with a peephole on top. Inside the box was a strip of film. It had photos of someone moving. **Spools** pulled the film along quickly. An electric lamp flashed on and off. The lamp lit up each photo so the person **peering** into the kinetoscope could see it.

The viewer's eye sent a signal to the brain. It told the brain that the figure was moving, so the viewer thought the figure really *was* moving. This special effect, or trick, was a key part of making moving pictures, or movies.

spools:

peering:

3 **Reread and Discuss** Reread the page. What made people think they saw pictures move when they looked in a kinetoscope? Cite text evidence in your discussion.

SHORT RESPONSE

Cite Text Evidence   Why does the author say that a key part of making movies was a "trick"? Cite details from the text in your response.

_____

_____

_____

_____

4 **Read** As you read, look for text evidence.

- Circle the name of the person shown in the photo.
- Underline a sentence that explains what westerns often were about.

Movie Magic!

Hollywood:

By the early 1900s, **Hollywood** was becoming the world's movie capital. At the same time, westerns were becoming the most popular movies. Westerns often told stories about cowboys, horses, and the wide-open plains.

But, in fact, many westerns were filmed in Hollywood **studios**!

studios:

The actor John Wayne starred in many Hollywood movies.

5 **Reread** Reread the page. Why does this section have the heading "Movie Magic!"? Cite text evidence in your response.

_____

_____

_____

6 Read As you read, look for text evidence.

- Circle the name of the diagram.
- Underline a sentence that describes one type of special effect.

Special Effects

Filmmakers today use special effects, just as Edison did. Some special effects make events seem real. A blue screen is one way to make people look like they are flying!

filmmakers:

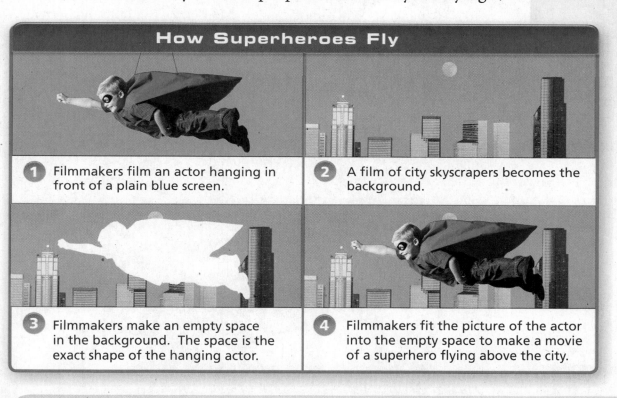

How Superheroes Fly

1. Filmmakers film an actor hanging in front of a plain blue screen.

2. A film of city skyscrapers becomes the background.

3. Filmmakers make an empty space in the background. The space is the exact shape of the hanging actor.

4. Filmmakers fit the picture of the actor into the empty space to make a movie of a superhero flying above the city.

7 Reread and Discuss Reread the page and study the diagram. Why is each box in the diagram numbered? Cite text evidence in your discussion.

SHORT RESPONSE

Cite Text Evidence How does the diagram help you understand how superheroes fly in a movie? Cite text evidence in your response.

_____

_____

Lesson Learned

Background Talented athletes seem to score baskets, hit baseballs, or soar through the air with almost no effort. But athletes depend on science to help them perform.

Setting a Purpose Read the text to learn about the science behind sports such as basketball and baseball.

Science for Sports Fans

by Alice Cary

CLOSE READ
Notes

① Read As you read, look for text evidence. Underline two sports activities that involve science.

rooting:

slam-dunks:

Think about science the next time you are **rooting** for your favorite team. Science is at work every time an athlete hits a home run or **slam-dunks** a basketball.

2 Read As you read, look for text evidence. Underline words that tell what happens as a result of pushing hard off a basketball court.

How high **professional** basketball players jump depends on how much force, or power, they use to push off the court. They jump higher when they push harder. As a result, they fly through the air longer. Scientists say that a player who jumps four feet to slam-dunk hangs in the air for one full second.

professional:

3 Reread and Discuss Reread the page. Why might basketball players be interested in learning about the science behind their sport? Cite text evidence in your discussion.

SHORT RESPONSE

Cite Text Evidence Based on the information on this page, what can you infer about a basketball player who jumps as high as four feet to slam-dunk a ball? Cite details from the text in your response.

_____

_____

_____

_____

④ **Read** As you read, look for text evidence.

- Circle the part of the picture that shows the first step for finding the sweet spot.
- In the text, underline the second step for finding the sweet spot.

Where Is the Sweet Spot?

sweet spot:

Do you want to win a baseball championship? You can send the ball flying if you hit it with the bat's **sweet spot**. To find it, get a wooden baseball bat and a hammer. Then follow these steps.

1. Hold the bat between your thumb and index finger, just below the knob.
2. Have a friend use the hammer to tap the bat, starting at the bottom and moving up inch by inch.

vibrate:

3. The entire bat should **vibrate** with each tap, but you won't feel a thing when your friend taps the sweet spot.

What's Happening?

The bat hardly vibrates when you hit the ball at the sweet spot. Instead, more energy goes into the baseball, sending it farther.

⑤ **Reread** Reread the page. According to step three of the directions, how can you tell where the sweet spot is on the bat? Cite text evidence in your response.

_____

_____

6 Read As you read, look for text evidence.

- Circle the words that tell what this section of the text is about.
- Underline the first step in doing an ollie.

Mastering the Ollie

Every skateboard competitor knows how to do an ollie. This trick allows skaters to jump over things. When **airborne**, the board seems glued to their feet.

This trick isn't magic. It's science. A skater pushes down with one foot on the back of the board when he or she jumps. This **force** raises the front of the board.

Next, the skater pushes the front of the board down. As the skateboard levels, the skater seems to fly through the air without losing contact with the board.

airborne:

force:

7 Reread and Discuss Reread the page. How does the author organize the steps for doing an ollie? Cite text evidence in your discussion.

SHORT RESPONSE

Cite Text Evidence Why does the author say the ollie is science, not magic? How does the author prove this is true? Cite text evidence in your response.

_____

_____

_____

_____

_____

Background Some people have gardens in their backyard. Some have tiny gardens on their windowsill. Community gardens are special because they are shared by a group of people working side by side.

Setting a Purpose Read the text to learn why and how people create community gardens.

Goodness Grows in Gardens

by Tina Brigham

① **Read** As you read, look for text evidence.

- Circle the title of this text.
- Underline a sentence that tells who tends, or takes care of, community gardens.

Community gardens come in many shapes and sizes. They are found in big cities, suburbs, and small country towns. These gardens are tended by people of all ages. Some gardeners grow beautiful flowers, but many choose to grow food. There are good reasons for having community gardens.

② Read As you read, look for text evidence.

- Circle the words that tell what the text on this page is about.
- Underline a question that the rest of the text answers. Then underline one answer to the question.

Good for You

grocery:

You know that fruits and vegetables are good for you. You can buy these foods in **grocery** stores, so why take the trouble to grow them yourself? Instead of sitting inside while other people grow the food you eat, you can enjoy being outdoors. Growing a garden is a lot of work, so you get lots of exercise. Many people say they are more excited about eating food that they have grown themselves.

③ Reread and Discuss Reread the page. Why might people be more likely to eat food that comes from a community garden? Cite text evidence in your discussion.

SHORT RESPONSE

Cite Text Evidence What useful information does the heading give you about the text on this page? Cite details from the text in your response.

_____

_____

_____

_____

_____

4 **Read** As you read, look for text evidence.

- Circle the words that tell what this section of the text is about.
- Underline details that tell two places where community gardens can be found.

Good for Communities

There are thousands of community gardens in the United States. They can be found in cities like Boston, Massachusetts, and small towns like Winter Garden, Florida. Wherever they are, community gardens help people make new friends and grow good food to eat. Gardens improve communities by turning empty or **overgrown** plots of land into something useful and attractive. Children and adults work together and learn from one another. **Volunteer** gardeners provide food for those in need.

overgrown:

volunteer:

5 **Reread** Reread the page. What are two ways community gardens are good for communities? Cite text evidence in your response.

_____

_____

_____

6 Read As you read, look for text evidence.

- Circle the words that tell what this section of the text is about.
- Underline the words that tell about the photo.

Good for Our Country

In the spring of 2009, a community garden sprang up at the White House. The White House is the official home of the President. Soon after Barack Obama and his family moved into the White House, Mrs. Obama decided to plant a garden. Everyone would share the garden, and that meant sharing the work that went with it. Even the President would have to help.

White House gardeners **prepared** the land, and elementary students from Washington, D.C., helped Mrs. Obama to plant seeds. They planted carrots, potatoes, strawberries, tomatoes, and other foods. The White House Kitchen Garden has fed the President and his family, special guests, and also homeless families in Washington, D.C. Our nation's Kitchen Garden has set a good example for others to follow.

prepared:

Mrs. Obama believes it is important to get children involved in growing fresh fruit and vegetables.

7 Reread and Discuss Reread the page. What can you learn from the photo that you can't learn from the caption? Cite text evidence in your discussion.

SHORT RESPONSE

Cite Text Evidence   Why do you think it is important for everyone to share the work that goes into caring for the White House Kitchen Garden? Cite evidence from the text in your response.

_____

_____

The Trail of Tears

by Samuel Winters

① Read As you read, look for text evidence. Circle the title of this text. Then circle the words that tell about this section of the text.

The Cherokee Homeland

In 1830, the Cherokee lived in the southeast part of the United States. White settlers wanted Cherokee land. They wanted it to farm. They wanted to look for gold on it. Why? People had found gold in Georgia. Most of the gold was on Cherokee land.

(2) **Read** As you read, look for text evidence.

- Circle the words that tell what the text on this page is about.
- Underline a sentence that explains how the Indian Removal Act hurt Native Americans.

Loss of Land

The U.S. government passed a law in 1830 called the Indian Removal Act. The law let the President give land to Native Americans. The land was west of the Mississippi River. In return, Native Americans would give up their land in the east. Then white settlers could have it.

In 1835, a small group of Cherokee signed a **treaty**. They sold their land to the U.S. government. They would move west. Most Cherokee did not want to give up their land, but the U.S. government said the treaty meant that all Cherokee had to move.

treaty:

(3) **Reread and Discuss** Reread the page. What does the heading tell you about the main idea of the text? Cite text evidence in your discussion.

SHORT RESPONSE

Cite Text Evidence How did the Indian Removal Act help settlers? Cite details from the text.

_____

_____

_____

© Houghton Mifflin Harcourt Publishing Company

4 **Read** As you read, look for text evidence.

- Circle the date that tells when the Cherokee moved.
- Underline a word that tells you the Cherokee did not want to move.

The Hard Journey

In 1838, the U.S. Army forced about sixteen thousand Cherokee from their homes. They left the farms they had tended fondly. They moved to what is now Oklahoma. Some went by boat. Most of them marched.

Parts of the trail were steep and **rugged**. Women carried their babies over each mountain peak. The weak and very young rode. Mist swirled around them. Rain and snow lashed at them. The Cherokee marched on, pausing only briefly for rest. Many people became ill. They had little food. Thousands died. The Cherokee **pleaded** with the soldiers to stop long enough to allow them to bury those who had died.

rugged:

pleaded:

5 **Reread** Reread the page. What details tell you the U.S. Army soldiers probably did not treat the Cherokee well? Cite text evidence in your response.

_____

_____

_____

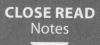
6 Read As you read, look for text evidence.

- Circle the name of the trail that is written on the map.
- Underline the text that tells about the map.

A **survivor** told what the sad journey was like. "Children cry and many men cry. . . . Many days pass and people die. . . ." The Cherokee reached Oklahoma in the winter. They called the hard journey The Trail Where They Cried.

survivor:

The U.S. government created the Trail of Tears National Historic Trail in 1987 to honor the Cherokee. It stretches for 2,200 miles across nine states.

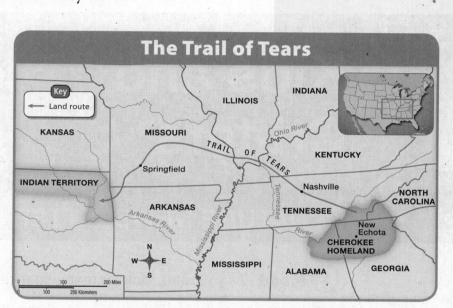

The Trail of Tears

Key
← Land route

KANSAS

MISSOURI

Springfield

ILLINOIS

INDIANA

Ohio River

KENTUCKY

INDIAN TERRITORY

ARKANSAS

Arkansas River

TRAIL OF TEARS

Tennessee

Nashville

TENNESSEE

NORTH CAROLINA

New Echota

CHEROKEE HOMELAND

MISSISSIPPI

ALABAMA

GEORGIA

N W E S

0 100 200 Miles
0 100 200 Kilometers

This map shows the route the Cherokee traveled in 1838. What made the journey so difficult?

7 Reread and Discuss Reread the page and look at the map. What can you learn from the small map at the top right of the bigger map?

SHORT RESPONSE

Cite Text Evidence Why is it important to get information from both the text and the map to understand what happened to the Cherokee? Cite text evidence in your response.

_____

_____

_____

Background 4-H is a group for kids all across the United States. The four *H*s stand for *head*, *heart*, *hands*, and *health*. Kids in 4-H do all kinds of activities in their communities. You'll read about some of them ahead!

Setting a Purpose Read the text to find out how 4-H members get involved with animals and nature.

Kids and Critters

A NATURE NEWSLETTER

① **Read** As you read, look for text evidence.

- Circle the title. Then circle the words that tell about this section of the text.
- Underline a sentence that tells where you can find 4-H programs.

What Is 4-H?

4-H is a program for boys and girls ages eight to eighteen. In a 4-H club, you'll make new friends and find new interests. You might care for animals, work with partners to plant a community garden, or patrol a park to pick up litter. You'll learn the 4-H motto, "To Make the Best Better."

All fifty states have 4-H programs. Look for a club near you.

(2) **Read** As you read, look for text evidence.

- Circle the words that tell what the two text sections on this page are about.
- Underline a sentence that tells how to care for a pet rabbit.

Get the Rabbit Habit

4-H boys and girls in Bell County, Texas, have the rabbit habit. Each year they show their rabbits at 4-H fairs.

You don't need any special skill or ability to care for a rabbit. Just give your pet plenty of love, food, and water, and a clean, cozy place to live. Your rabbit will quiver its nose with delight!

A City Nature Walk

There's so much to see on a city nature walk. Your 4-H leader can supervise the walk. Be **attentive** to what you see. You may spot a bird's nest, some squirrels, or even a coyote!

attentive:

(3) **Reread and Discuss** Reread the page. What do both sections of the text have in common? Cite text evidence in your discussion.

SHORT RESPONSE

Cite Text Evidence Why are there two different headings for the text on this page? How are they useful? Cite details from the text in your response.

_____

_____

_____

_____

shift:

shelter:

Use What You Learn!

In 4-H, you use what you learn to help your community. Maybe you can use what you learn about animals to work a **shift** in a local animal **shelter**.

Shelter animals can't spend all day lying in their cages. They need exercise and attention. By walking dogs or cuddling cats, a loyal volunteer can make a big difference. With your help, an animal that used to be shy can become a friendly tail-wagger!

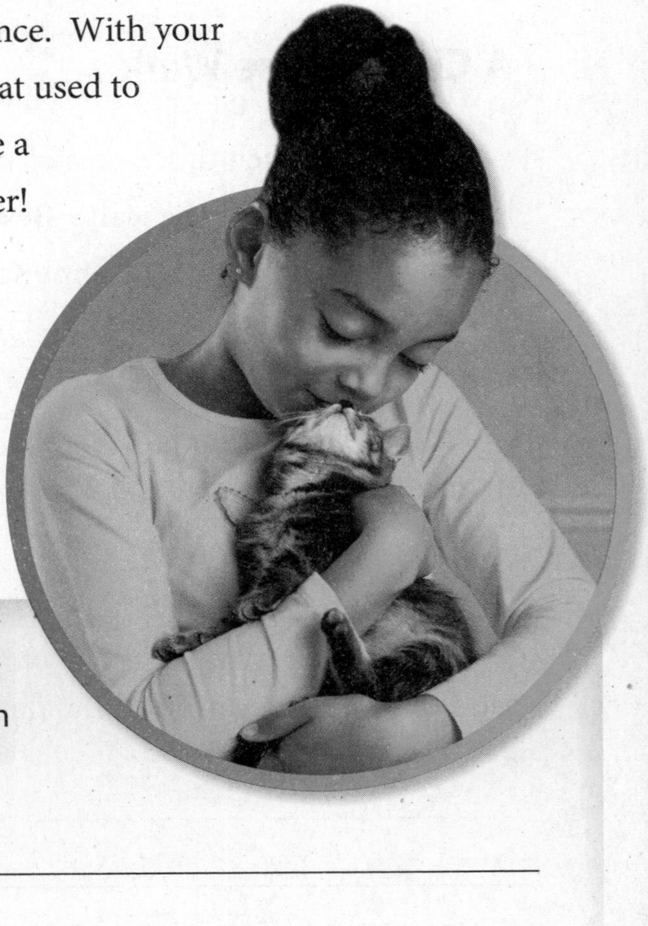

_____

_____

_____

6 Read As you read, look for text evidence.

- Circle the words that tell the name of the event.
- Underline a detail that tells where the event will take place.

Summer Fair

August 10, at 1:00 P.M.
Juniper Park

Do not miss this exciting summer event!

- **Groom** your pet.
- Pick your biggest tomato.
- Choose something you've made.
- Show off your hard work!

Blue ribbons in these groups:

Animals
Vegetables
Handicrafts

groom:

7 Reread and Discuss Reread the page. What is the purpose of the information on this page? Cite text evidence in your discussion.

SHORT RESPONSE

Cite Text Evidence How does the Summer Fair share the goals of 4-H? Cite text evidence from this page and the rest of the text in your response.

_____

_____

_____

Imagine a Recipe

by Cameron Hart

① **Read** As you read, look for text evidence.

- Circle the title of this text.
- Underline two details about how chefs create and use recipes.

Being a chef is a lot like being an artist. A chef's materials are the foods in a kitchen. To be a chef, you need to express yourself in many different ways. Chefs combine flavors that taste delicious. They present food that smells good and that looks good, too.

Sometimes, chefs use their imaginations to make up a recipe for a new dish. At other times, they start with a recipe that has been around for ages. Then they change a few ingredients or cook it in a different way.

②Read As you read, look for text evidence.

- Circle the title of the recipe.
- Underline the first two ingredients in the recipe.

You can be a chef in your own kitchen. Follow the steps in this recipe to make flan. Flan is a popular dessert in many Spanish-speaking countries, including Puerto Rico. The **traditional** flavor is caramel. There are also different flavors, such as orange or vanilla. Use your imagination to add flavor and make this recipe your own.

traditional:

PUERTO RICAN FLAN

Ingredients:
1 c. sugar
4 eggs
1 (14 oz.) can condensed milk
1 3/4 c. water
1/4 tsp. salt
1 tsp. vanilla or other flavoring

③Reread and Discuss Reread the page. What does the text tell you about flan? Cite text evidence in your discussion.

SHORT RESPONSE

Cite Text Evidence   What kinds of information are on the recipe card? Why do you need this information to make flan? Cite details from the text.

_____

_____

_____

_____

_____

4 **Read** As you read, look for text evidence.

- Circle the step that tells what to do first when you make the recipe.
- Underline the words that tell what to do after you pour the mixture through a strainer.

1. Ask an adult to heat the oven to 350 degrees.

2. Have an adult help you slowly melt the sugar until it is the color of caramel. Swirl the melted sugar onto the sides of a pie dish. Then set the dish on a wire rack.

strainer:

3. Mix the other ingredients in a bowl. Pour the mixture through a **strainer** to make it smooth. Then pour it into the dish.

5 **Reread** Reread the page. Why are the steps in the recipe numbered? Cite text evidence in your response.

_____

_____

_____

⑥ **Read** As you read, look for text evidence.

- Circle the text that tells what to do before you put the pie dish in the oven.

- Underline the text that tells what to do right after you take the pie dish out of the oven.

4. Pour warm water into a large baking pan until it is about one inch deep. Set the pie dish in the warm water. Have an adult help you put the whole thing in the oven. Bake for one hour.

5. Have an adult help you take the pie dish out of the oven. Let it cool and then put it in the refrigerator. When the flan is cold, carefully turn the flan onto a plate and serve in slices.

⑦ **Reread and Discuss** Reread the page. What would happen to the flan if you skipped step 4 of the recipe? Cite text evidence in your discussion.

SHORT RESPONSE

Cite Text Evidence Why should a new chef follow this recipe exactly as it is written? Why can an experienced chef imagine a new way to make it? Cite text evidence from this page and the rest of the text in your response.

_____

_____

_____

_____

UNIT 4
Natural Wonders

Background Judy Moody is a character from a series of books by Megan McDonald. Each book shows Judy trying to solve problems in funny, sometimes silly, ways. These made-up stories are all examples of humorous fiction. In this story, Judy comes up with a pretty silly—and smelly—idea for a pet!

Setting a Purpose Read to find out what is funny about Judy Moody's favorite pet.

My Smelly Pet
from *Judy Moody*

by Megan McDonald   illustrated by Peter H. Reynolds

1 **Read** As you read, look for text evidence.

- Circle the paragraph that tells Judy's main problem.
- Underline two sentences that describe how she solves this problem.

For a collage about herself, Judy Moody needs to show her favorite pet. Judy's family has one pet, an old cat named Mouse. Judy said that Mouse can't be her favorite pet if she is their only pet. Her parents agree to take her
5   to the pet store.

At the store, Judy finds a strange little plant. The store assistant explains that it is a Venus flytrap. Even though it is a plant, it eats insects such as flies and ants. Back at home, Judy and her little brother, Stink, feed the plant too
10   much. Judy takes it to school the next day anyway, hoping that it will digest its meal in time for Share and Tell.

Tomorrow morning came. The jaws were still closed. Judy tried teasing it with a brand new ant. "Here you go," she said in her best squeaky baby voice. "You like ants,
15   don't you?" The jaws did not open one tiny centimeter. The plant did not move one trigger hair.

2 **Reread** Reread the page. What does Judy do with her new pet that shows she can be silly? Cite evidence from the text.

_____

_____

_____

67

3 **Read** As you read, look for text evidence.

- Circle two sentences that tell what Judy's next problem is.
- Underline two sentences that describe two solutions that Rocky thinks of.

On the bus, Judy showed Rocky her new pet. "I couldn't wait to show everybody how it eats. Now it won't even move. And it smells."

20 "Open Sesame!" said Rocky, trying some magic words. Nothing happened.

"Maybe," said Rocky, "the bus will bounce it open."

"Maybe," said Judy. But even the bouncing of the bus did not make her new pet open up.

25 "If this thing dies, I'm stuck with Mouse for MY FAVORITE PET," Judy said.

Mr. Todd said first thing, "Okay, class, take out your Me **collage** folders. I'll pass around old magazines, and you can spend the next half-hour cutting out pictures for

30 your collages. You still have over three weeks, but I'd like to see how everybody's doing."

collage:

4 **Reread** Reread the page. What can you infer about Rocky's character? Cite details in your response.

_____

_____

_____

68

5 **Read** As you read, look for text evidence.

- Circle a sentence that describes one more problem for Judy.
- Underline the text that shows Judy's problems are getting worse.

Her Me collage folder! Judy had been so busy with her
new pet, she had forgotten to bring her folder to school.

Judy Moody **sneaked** a peek at Frank Pearl's folder.

sneaked:

35 He had cut out pictures of macaroni (favorite food?), ants
(favorite pet?), and shoes. Shoes? Frank Pearl's best
friend was a pair of shoes?

Judy looked down at the open backpack under her
desk. The jaws were still closed. Now her whole

40 backpack was smelly. Judy took the straw from her juice
box and poked at the Venus flytrap. No luck. It would
never open in time for Share and Tell!

6 **Reread and Discuss** Reread the page. How are Frank Pearl's
ideas for his Me collage similar to and different from Judy's idea for a
favorite pet? Cite evidence from the story in your discussion.

SHORT RESPONSE

Cite Text Evidence How do events in the story make Judy feel?
Cite text evidence in your response.

_____

_____

_____

_____

_____

CLOSE READ
Notes

7 Read As you read, look for text evidence.

- Circle text that shows Judy is not paying attention to Frank's questions.
- Underline something Frank says that describes Judy's problem in a funny way.

"Well?" Frank asked.

"Well, what?"

45 "Are you going to come?"

"Where?"

"My birthday party. A week from Saturday. All the boys from our class are coming. And Adrian and Sandy from next door."

50 Judy Moody did not care if the president himself was coming. She sniffed her backpack. It stunk like a skunk!

"What's in your backpack?" Frank asked.

"None of your **beeswax**," Judy said.

beeswax:

"It smells like dead tuna fish!" Frank Pearl said. Judy
55 hoped her Venus flytrap would come back to life and bite Frank Pearl before he ever had another birthday.

Mr. Todd came over. "Judy, you haven't cut out any pictures. Do you have your folder?"

"I did—I mean—it was—then—well—no," said Judy.

60 "I got a new pet last night."

8 Reread Reread the page. Which details help make the story silly?

_____

_____

_____

⑨ Read As you read, look for text evidence.

- Mr. Todd makes a joke about what happened to Judy's Me folder. Circle the sentences that show Mr. Todd's joke.
- Underline two sentences that show how Judy feels.

"Don't tell me," said Mr. Todd. "Your new pet ate your Me collage folder."

"Not exactly. But it did eat one dead fly and one live ant. And then a big glob of . . ."

65   "Next time try to remember to bring your folder to school, Judy. And please, everyone, keep homework away from animals!"

"My new pet's not an animal, Mr. Todd," Judy said. "And it doesn't eat homework. Just bugs and **raw**

70 hamburger." She pulled the Venus flytrap from her backpack. Judy could not believe her eyes! Its arm was no longer droopy. The stuck trap was now wide open, and her plant was looking hungry.

"It's MY FAVORITE PET," said Judy. "Meet Jaws!"

raw:

⑩ Reread and Discuss Reread the page. How does Judy's mood change by the end of the story? What events help to change her mood? Cite text evidence in your discussion.

SHORT RESPONSE

(*Cite Text Evidence*) What is funny about Judy's favorite pet? Cite text evidence in your response.

_____

_____

_____

Finding Fossils for Fun

by Alice Cary

① **Read** As you read, look for text evidence.

- Circle the title of this text.
- Underline the words that tell what kind of fossil some kids found in Florida.

Have you ever hunted for fossils? People often find them by accident. In 2007, a Florida high school student and her friends went to a creek to take photos for a school project. They saw lots of bones in the water. The girls were surprised! They had found the remains of an Ice Age mammoth.

Scientists began digging at the creek. Soon they were uncovering other animal skeletons.

2 Read As you read, look for text evidence.

- Circle the word that tells what the text on this page is about.
- Underline a sentence that gives a definition of fossils.

Fossils

remains:

Fossils are evidence of ancient life. Sometimes dirt or sand covers leaves and bones. Layers of dirt and sand protect these **remains** from damage. The layers build up as time passes. After many years, the remains harden and become fossils.

You may find fossils buried near you! The chart on the next page gives you tips for hunting them.

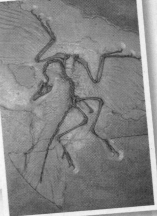

3 Reread and Discuss Reread the page. What happens to old leaves and bones over a long time? Cite text evidence in your discussion.

SHORT RESPONSE

Cite Text Evidence Why don't all leaves and bones become fossils? Cite details from the text in your response.

_____

_____

_____

_____

④ **Read** As you read, look for text evidence.

- Circle the title of the chart.
- Underline the places you can look for fossils.

Hunting Guide

chisel:

impressions:

Where to Look	What to Hunt	Tools	Searching Tips
layers of rock	eggs, nests	hammer and **chisel**	Work carefully so you don't miss anything.
layers of sand or mud	footprints, leaf **impressions**	notebook, pen, camera	Take notes to keep track of where each discovery was found.
deserts, canyons, cliffs, hills, and mountains	shells	plastic box or newspapers and rubber bands for carrying finds	Look for things that seem unusual or out of place.

⑤ **Reread** Reread the chart. What are the four kinds of information the chart tells about? Cite text evidence in your response.

_____

_____

_____

6 Read As you read, look for text evidence.

- Circle the rules for hunting fossils safely.
- Underline words that tell when David looked for fossils.

You're never too young to find fossils. David Shiffler loved **fierce** dinosaurs. In 1995, when he was only three years old, David dug up a green rock. He called it a dinosaur egg.

David's father took the rock to a museum a few months later. David was right! He had found a piece of dinosaur egg! Scientists could prove it. The egg was about 150 million years old!

fierce:

File   Edit   View   Favorites   Tools   Help

Hunt Fossils Safely

- Take an adult.
- Choose a safe location.
- Get permission to hunt before you start.
- Wear safety glasses.

COOL CLICKS!

Museums with Fossils

Fossils in the News

Fossil Finds

7 Reread and Discuss Reread the page. What is the first rule for hunting fossils safely? Why do you think it's important? Cite text evidence in your discussion.

SHORT RESPONSE

Cite Text Evidence   If this were a real website, what could you learn by clicking on the Cool Clicks? Can you find some of that information in this text? Cite text evidence from this page and the rest of the text in your response.

_____

_____

_____

Background Robert Frost was a famous American poet. He lived from 1874 to 1963 and spent many years in New England. Frost wrote many poems about nature and living in the country.

Setting a Purpose Read the poem to learn the poet's feelings about a forest in winter.

Stopping by Woods on a Snowy Evening

by Robert Frost

① Read As you read, look for text evidence.

- Circle the title of the poem.
- Underline the words that rhyme in the first stanza, or section, of the poem.

Whose woods these are I think I know.
His house is in the village though;
He will not see me stopping here
To watch his woods fill up with snow.

My little horse must think it queer
To stop without a farmhouse near
Between the woods and frozen lake
The darkest evening of the year.

2 **Read** As you read, look for text evidence.

- Circle two lines that are repeated in the poem.
- Underline the words that rhyme in the first stanza on this page.

He gives his **harness** bells a shake
To ask if there is some mistake.
The only other sound's the sweep
Of easy wind and **downy** flake.

The woods are lovely, dark and deep,
But I have promises to keep,
And miles to go before I sleep,
And miles to go before I sleep.

harness:

downy:

3 **Reread and Discuss** Reread the page. What words does the poet use to describe the woods? Do you think he likes the woods or thinks they are scary? Cite text evidence in your discussion.

SHORT RESPONSE

Cite Text Evidence What are two ways the last stanza of the poem is different from the ones that come before it? Why do you think the poet made it different? Cite details from the text in your response.

_____

_____

_____

_____

Background Wild animals such as squirrels and raccoons have always lived in urban areas. But today bears and other surprising animals are appearing in town and city parks, streets, and yards.

Setting a Purpose Read the text to learn about sharing the environment with wild creatures.

Whose Land Is It?

by Ellen Gold

① Read As you read, look for text evidence.

- Circle the words that tell about this section of the text.
- Underline the sentence that tells one thing both people and animals need.

People and Wild Animals

People and animals need places to live. Animals have lived in the wilderness for thousands of years. They live in ancient forests, oceans, and other habitats. Yet wild animals also live in people's yards. They live in cities, too.

② Read As you read, look for text evidence.

- Circle the words that tell about this section of the text.
- Underline a sentence that tells the main reason wild animals are moving into cities and towns.

Habitat Loss

Why are wild animals moving closer to people? They are losing their habitats. Then they must find new places to live.

Fires destroy many animals' homes. Some years are especially fiery. In 2006, fires burned nearly 10 million acres of wild land in the United States.

People destroy habitats, too. People build homes, stores, and roads where wild animals live. In Florida, many homes are near swamps and **waterways**. These are places where alligators live.

waterways:

③ Reread and Discuss Reread the page. How do fires affect animals' habitats? Cite text evidence in your discussion.

SHORT RESPONSE

Cite Text Evidence How does the photo connect to the main text? Cite details from the text in your response.

_____

_____

_____

4 **Read** As you read, look for text evidence.

- Circle the words that give more information about the photo.
- Underline a sentence that explains why alligators and people don't usually live near each other.

Changing Ways

prehistoric:

Alligators have been around since **prehistoric** times. They mostly fear people. Yet that may be changing. Why is this?

The reason is far from mysterious. Some people feed alligators. Then those alligators stop fearing people. They may think that all people will feed them.

Running into an unexpected alligator can be horrifying. People may have to take emergency steps, like having a trapper catch the animal.

5 **Reread** Reread the page. What information can you get from the photo caption that you can't get from the photo or the main text? Cite text evidence in your response.

_____

_____

_____

6 Read As you read, look for text evidence.

- Circle the words in the caption that tell where the bear is.
- Underline a sentence that tells a way that city bears are different from country bears.

Other animals **link** people to food, too. Scientific experts know a lot about black bears. Country bears look for food during the day. City bears eat at night. They know that people put out garbage. So, city bears find food in dumpsters and trashcans.

How can people keep bears away? People need to change their habits. They should use bear-proof trashcans. They should fasten the cans immediately after use. If bears can't get food, they won't come back.

link:

This black bear has wandered into someone's backyard garden, right in the heart of a big city. Have wild animals ever visited your home?

7 Reread and Discuss Reread the page. How is the information on this page similar to the information on page 80? Cite text evidence in your discussion.

SHORT RESPONSE

Cite Text Evidence What advice does the author give to people who don't want bears around? Do you think this is good advice? Why or why not? Cite text evidence from this page and the rest of the text in your response.

_____

_____

_____

_____

Background This myth comes from the Inuit, a Native American group that lives in Alaska, Canada, and other northern parts of the world. The main character of this myth is a raven, a big black bird that is a lot like a crow. The myth is told in the form of a play.

Setting a Purpose Read the play to learn what the raven does to help the people.

The Raven: An Inuit Myth

retold by Peter Case

① **Read** As you read, look for text evidence.

- Circle the text feature that gives the names of the characters.
- Underline words that tell when the events take place.

Cast of Characters

Narrator   **Old Man**   **Person**   **Raven**

Narrator: Long ago, the People lived in darkness. There was no sun to help things grow. The People called to Raven for help.

Person: Oh, Raven, help us. Our lives are a constant struggle.

② **Read** As you read, look for text evidence.

- Circle the words that tell why Raven goes to find the Old Man.
- Underline words that tell what Raven does as soon as he gets to the shelter.

Raven: I have heard of an Old Man who has two glowing globes of light. I will try to get these globes.

Narrator: Raven went **gliding** over the dark wilderness. He came to the shelter where the Old Man lived with his daughter. There, Raven turned himself into a human child.

gliding:

Old Man: I have a grandson! How wonderful!

Narrator: Raven spoke in the voice of a small child.

Raven: May I please play with the globes of light?

Old Man: Here, grandson, you can play with them.

③ **Reread and Discuss** Reread the page. What is the narrator's role in the play? Cite text evidence in your discussion.

SHORT RESPONSE

Cite Text Evidence What character traits does Raven show when he goes to see the Old Man? Cite details from the text in your response.

_____

_____

_____

_____

4 Read As you read, look for text evidence.

- Circle the narrator's words on this page.
- Underline the reason Raven says he wants to take the globes outside.

overheated:

Narrator: Raven thought of a trick to steal the globes. He pretended he was **overheated** inside the warm shelter.

Raven: It's so hot inside. I want to take the globes outside.

Old Man: Yes, grandson. You can play outside with the globes.

Narrator: Once Raven was outside, he put on his layer of feathers and flew off with the globes.

5 Reread Reread the page. Why does Raven trick the Old Man? Cite text evidence in your response.

_____

_____

_____

6 **Read** As you read, look for text evidence.

- Circle the words that tell what the globes of light turned into.
- Underline a sentence that tells how Raven's actions help the People.

Narrator: When he got back to the colony of People, Raven threw the globes up into the sky. One became the sun, and the other became the moon. The People were **overjoyed**.

Person: Now the **climate** will be good for growing food in this region of the world. Thank you, Raven, for the gift of the sun and for the unexpected gift of the moon.

overjoyed:

climate:

7 **Reread and Discuss** Reread the page and think back to the rest of the play. Why does the Person call the moon "unexpected"? Cite text evidence in your discussion.

SHORT RESPONSE

Cite Text Evidence According to this myth, what part of nature does Raven create? Are Raven's actions in the myth more good than bad? Why do you think so? Cite text evidence in your response.

_____

_____

_____

UNIT 5
Going Places

Background The Oregon Trail was a dirt road that was 2,170 miles long. It started in Missouri and ended in Oregon, on the West Coast of the United States. Pioneers took the Oregon Trail to reach the West.

Setting a Purpose Read the text to learn how pioneers traveled across the United States.

Wagons of the Old West

by Maria Santos   **illustrated by Dan Bridy**

(1) **Read** As you read, look for text evidence.

- Circle the title of this text. Then circle the words that tell about one section of text on this page.
- Underline the words that explain what a wagon is.

One of the oldest kinds of transportation is the wagon. It is a four-wheeled vehicle drawn by strong animals. People around the world have driven wagons for thousands of years.

Wagons on the Oregon Trail

In the United States, wagons made history between the 1830s and 1860s. During this time, thousands of pioneers traveled westward. Some went as far as Oregon, but others settled in many places along the way.

(2) **Read** As you read, look for text evidence.

- Circle words that tell how long a journey to the West Coast might take.
- Underline words that tell what families took on their trip across the country.

The pioneers journeyed for up to six months to reach the West Coast. They had to pack a lot of food and supplies for the trip. Families packed some of their furniture, too. To protect their **possessions** and supplies from the sun and the rain, they used covered wagons.

Back east, there was an enormous wagon known as the Conestoga wagon. Its rear wheels were as tall as a man. The top rose to more than 11 feet above the ground. The back and front of the wagon bed were sloped upward so that **cargo** would not tip out when traveling across mountains.

possessions:

cargo:

(3) **Reread and Discuss** Reread the page. Why did pioneers use covered wagons? Cite text evidence in your discussion.

SHORT RESPONSE

Cite Text Evidence What made the Conestoga wagon especially useful for traveling across the country? Cite details from the text in your response.

_____

_____

_____

_____

④ **Read** As you read, look for text evidence.

- Circle words that explain a problem with the Conestoga wagon.
- Underline words that tell what the prairie schooner looked similar to.

People liked the design of the Conestoga, but these wagons were too heavy for the long journey west. They needed as many as six or eight horses to pull them. The wagons would have to travel over very rough land as there were no roads yet.

A smaller wagon was built, with high, sloped ends to keep its cargo from spilling out. It also had a white **canvas** cover to protect the cargo from sun and rain. Traveling in groups, or "trains," across the flat land of the prairies with their white tops, the wagons sometimes looked like ships. People soon called them "prairie schooners," as a schooner was a type of ship with white sails.

canvas:

⑤ **Reread** Reread the page. How was the prairie schooner similar to and different from the Conestoga wagon? Cite text evidence in your response.

_____

_____

_____

6 Read As you read the diagram, look for text evidence.

- Circle the name of the wagon the diagram shows.
- Underline labels that name parts of the wagon top.

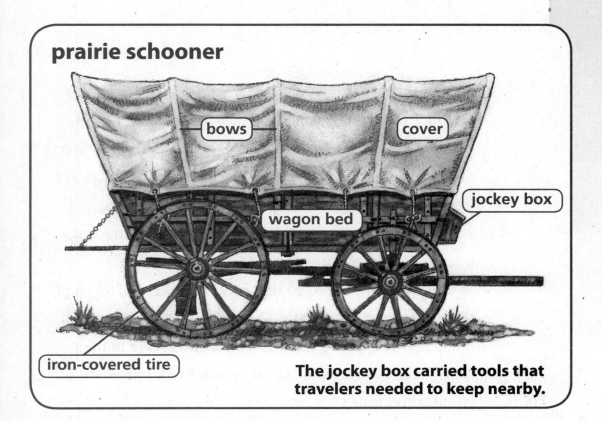

prairie schooner

bows

cover

jockey box

wagon bed

iron-covered tire

The jockey box carried tools that travelers needed to keep nearby.

7 Reread and Discuss Reread the page. What details can you learn from the caption that you can't learn from the diagram labels? Cite text evidence in your discussion.

SHORT RESPONSE

Cite Text Evidence How does the diagram help you understand more about the prairie schooner than you learned in the main text? Cite text evidence in your response.

_____

_____

_____

8 **Read** As you read, look for text evidence.

- Circle words that tell why pioneers no longer needed to carry heavy loads.
- Underline words that tell two ways springs were useful on wagons.

loads:

brace:

Once the pioneers chose a place to settle, they built houses to sleep in and to store their food. They no longer needed to carry such heavy **loads**. The prairie schooners were much too big for everyday use. Pioneers needed a wagon that was comfortable to ride on. Much smaller farm wagons were built.

Springs were added so that riders would not feel all of the bumps along the trails. A spring is a steel **brace** that holds up the bed of a wagon. The springs were lighter than the heavy frame of a prairie schooner, so the wagon could travel faster.

9 **Reread** Reread the page. What were the main ways farm wagons were different from prairie schooners? Cite text evidence in your response.

_____

_____

_____

10 **Read** As you read the diagram, look for text evidence.

- Circle the name of the wagon the diagram shows.
- Underline the label that names the part for holding cargo.

spring wagon

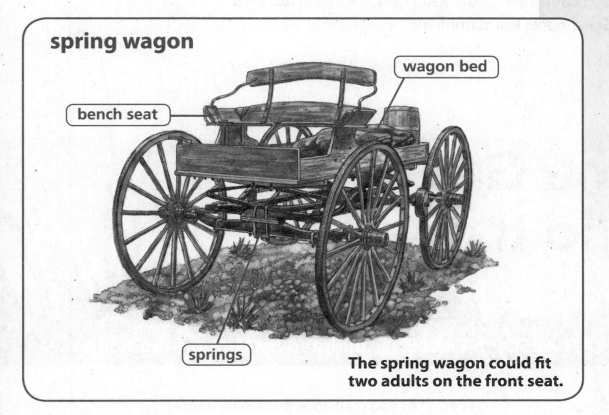

wagon bed

bench seat

springs

The spring wagon could fit two adults on the front seat.

11 **Reread and Discuss** Reread the page. What part of the wagon does the caption tell about? What can you learn from the caption that you can't tell from the rest of the diagram? Cite text evidence in your discussion.

SHORT RESPONSE

Cite Text Evidence Look back at both diagrams in the text. Which parts of the two wagons are similar? Which are different? Cite text evidence in your response.

_____

_____

_____

Background Fables are short stories. They often have animal characters and share a moral, or lesson. The fable you are about to read is by Aesop, a storyteller who lived very long ago.

Setting a Purpose Read the fable to find out what Grasshopper learns from Ant.

The Grasshopper and the Ant

AN AESOP'S FABLE **adapted by Margaretha Rabe**

① **Read** As you read, look for text evidence.

- Circle the title of the fable.
- Underline the activities that Grasshopper loves to do.

thunderous:

Grasshopper loved to sing and play his fiddle. He played quiet songs and **thunderous** tunes. Sometimes Grasshopper played frightening music. Then he would hop around in a dramatic way. That's when he caused accidents.

② **Read** As you read, look for text evidence.

- Circle a sentence that tells what happens when Grasshopper jumps into Ant's grain.
- Underline a word that shows Ant is annoyed when he talks to Grasshopper.

One time Grasshopper jumped into a pile of grain that Ant had spent all day **collecting**. The grain **scattered** across the **landscape**.

"You should be more careful, Grasshopper," scolded Ant. "I worked hard to gather that grain. Now I have to pile it up again."

"I'm sorry," said Grasshopper. "Why not take a break? It's a beautiful, sunny day. You'll have plenty of days to gather food."

collecting:

scattered:

landscape:

③ **Reread and Discuss** Reread the page. Why does Ant get annoyed with Grasshopper? How does Grasshopper react? Cite text evidence in your discussion.

SHORT RESPONSE

Cite Text Evidence Based on what you have read so far, how do you think Grasshopper and Ant are different? Cite details from the text in your response.

_____

_____

4 **Read** As you read, look for text evidence.

- Circle the words that tell why Ant thinks Grasshopper should get to work.
- Underline words that tell what Grasshopper plans to do when it gets cold.

survival:

migrate:

"You may think so, Grasshopper, but winter will soon be here. Then the ground will be frozen solid," said Ant. "Now is the time to gather food and plan for **survival**. You should take a break from playing and do some work."

Grasshopper said, "I'll **migrate** to someplace warm if it gets too chilly. That way, I can keep on playing and singing. But for now I'll play any song you like to make your work easier to do."

5 **Reread** Reread the page. Which of the characters is more worried about the future? Why? Cite text evidence in your response.

_____

_____

_____

6 Read As you read, look for text evidence.

- Circle words that tell why Grasshopper can't find food.
- Underline words that tell why Ant lets Grasshopper sing and play for him.

Weeks later, fat flakes of snow began to drift from the sky. Grasshopper **shivered**. It was so cold that he could hardly hold his fiddle. Grasshopper looked for food, but the ground had turned into a blanket of white snow.

"What will I do now? I can't find food, and it's too cold for me to go far. Maybe Ant will help me," thought Grasshopper.

Grasshopper **trudged** through the snow and knocked on Ant's door. "Will you give me food if I sing and play for you?" asked Grasshopper.

Ant said, "Yes I will. I worked hard the rest of the year, so now I have time to relax and have fun."

shivered:

trudged:

Moral: There are times to work and times to play.

7 Reread and Discuss Reread the page. Why does Grasshopper think Ant might be able to help him? Cite text evidence in your discussion.

SHORT RESPONSE

Cite Text Evidence Think about the story events and the story's moral. Based on these, which of the two characters is wiser? What makes you think so? Cite evidence from the text in your response.

_____

_____

_____

Today the United States Postal Service delivers billions of pieces of mail each year. Many, many people work hard to deliver mail to the right address at top speed. The mail service has come a long way since the early days, as you'll find out!

Setting a Purpose Read the text to learn about the history of the U.S. mail.

Moving the U.S. Mail

① **Read** As you read, look for text evidence.

- Circle the title. Then circle the heading that tells about the text on this page.
- Underline the words that tell who delivered mail in colonial times.

The United States Postal Service

The United States Postal Service has changed over the years. In colonial times, all kinds of people helped deliver mail. Sometimes letters managed to get through. Sometimes they didn't.

② **Read** As you read, look for text evidence.

- Circle the heading that tells about one section of text on this page.
- Underline a reason mail is now delivered faster.

Getting mail brings pleasure to many, but it has never been easy to deliver. Today the Postal Service makes a **sincere** effort to deliver all mail. Currently it delivers hundreds of millions of messages daily.

sincere:

Transportation Changes

Having conversations by mail has gotten much faster. Why is this? Transportation has improved. Long ago, people carried mail on foot, horseback, and **stagecoaches**. Today's mail is loaded onto trucks and planes.

stagecoaches:

③ **Reread and Discuss** Reread the page. Why has mail delivery improved so much? Cite text evidence in your discussion.

SHORT RESPONSE

Cite Text Evidence How has mail delivery changed from earlier times? How does this help people? Cite details from the text in your response.

_____

_____

_____

_____

4 **Read** As you read, look for text evidence.

- Circle the years on the timeline.
- Underline timeline text that tells about the fastest form of mail delivery.

Golden Moments of Mail History

inspired:

Gold was discovered in California in 1848. People rushed west. The California Gold Rush **inspired** faster mail delivery. It would be a long time until they could have a reunion with their families, so gold seekers wanted mail from home.

Pony Express riders carried mail to California in 1860 and 1861. Their rides could be full of terror. They faced blizzards

bandits:

and **bandits**.

By 1869 the Transcontinental Railroad linked railroads in the east with California. The mail moved faster than ever.

Delivery Times
New York to San Francisco

| 1800 | 1900 | 2000 |

Pony Express 13–14 days by train to Missouri, then on horseback

Transcontinental Railroad 7 days

Airplane 6–7 hours

5 **Reread** Look at the timeline. What two big improvements happened in mail delivery after the Pony Express? Which one is more recent? Cite details from the text in your response.

_____

_____

_____

_____

6 **Read** As you read, look for text evidence.
Circle a word that helps you understand the meaning
of *delayed*.

Each year around February 14, mail from around the
world takes a **detour**. This mail isn't slowed by blizzards
or bandits—it's delayed by love! In honor of Valentine's
Day, cards are mailed to the small town of Valentine,
Texas. They get the town's postmark and go on to their
final **destination**.

detour:

**Each year, in
Valentine, Texas,
the school holds
a design contest.
The city council
chooses the
loveliest design
to be used as that
year's postmark.**

destination:

LO♥E
LO♥E
LO♥E
LO♥E
LO♥E
USA 20 c

Aunt Susie
123 Msososo Street
Austin, TX 12307

7 **Reread and Discuss** Reread the page. What information can you
learn from the caption that you can't learn from the image of the envelope
or the main text? Cite text evidence in your discussion.

SHORT RESPONSE

Cite Text Evidence How is the information on this page different from
what you learned on earlier pages? Cite text evidence in your response.

_____

_____

_____

_____

The Land Volcanoes Built

by Patricia Ann Lynch

① Read As you read, look for text evidence.
- Circle the title of this text. Then circle the words that tell about one section of the text.
- Underline the definition of a volcano.

The islands of Hawaii spread over many miles of ocean. Eight large islands and 124 small ones are in the chain. Each island is really the top of a mountain that pokes out of the sea. How were these islands formed? The answer is *volcanoes*.

What Is a Volcano?

A volcano is an opening, or vent, that goes deep into Earth. Deep within Earth it is so hot that rock melts. The melted rock is called magma.

② **Read** As you read, look for text evidence.

- Circle name of the diagram.
- Underline the label that tells what happens after rock melts into magma.

erupts:

pressure:

Sometimes magma is pushed up and pours out of the volcano. Then the magma is called lava. The lava cools and hardens. It builds up. Over time, it can form a tall mountain. Each of the Hawaiian Islands formed in this way.

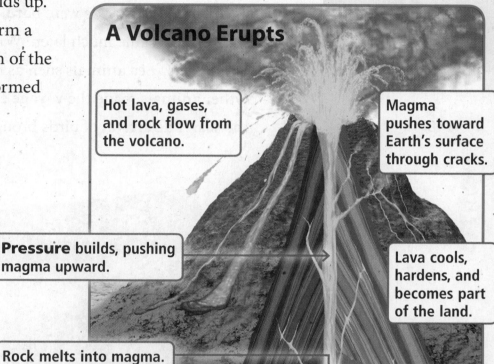

A Volcano Erupts

Hot lava, gases, and rock flow from the volcano.

Magma pushes toward Earth's surface through cracks.

Pressure builds, pushing magma upward.

Lava cools, hardens, and becomes part of the land.

Rock melts into magma.

③ **Reread and Discuss** Reread the text and diagram. What are the last two steps that happen when a volcano erupts? Cite text evidence in your discussion.

SHORT RESPONSE

Cite Text Evidence How does the diagram help you understand the main text? Cite details from the text in your response.

_____

_____

_____

© Houghton Mifflin Harcourt Publishing Company • Image Credits: ©Sam Clemens/Getty Images

4 **Read** As you read, look for text evidence.

- Circle the words that tell about this section of the text.
- Underline words that name the first kind of life that arrived in Hawaii.

bare:

voyage:

Life Arrives

At first, the islands were **bare**. Waves rippled on empty shores. Life came much later. Wind and water carried plant seeds. Sea animals such as monk seals swam there. Other animals made the **voyage** aboard objects floating in the sea. The arrival of birds brought song.

5 **Reread** Reread the page. What are three ways animals reached Hawaii? Cite text evidence in your response.

_____

_____

_____

6 **Read** As you read, look for text evidence.

- Circle the words that tell how the first people got to Hawaii.
- Underline ways that one kind of plant was useful to the first people in Hawaii.

The first people paddled in canoes from other islands. The stars guided them across the Pacific Ocean. The travelers spotted the islands. They dropped anchor in a calm bay and came ashore. The new islands were good places to live. There was plenty of fresh water to drink and lots of food. The leaves of the coconut tree could be used to build **thatched** shelters. Coconut **husks** could be twisted into strong ropes. These people became the first Hawaiians.

thatched:

husks:

People from China, Japan, Samoa, the Philippines, and other countries live in Hawaii today.

7 **Reread and Discuss** Reread the page. According to the author, why were the islands of Hawaii good places to live? Cite text evidence in your discussion.

SHORT RESPONSE

Cite Text Evidence The photo caption says that people from many countries live in Hawaii today. Based on this, what can you conclude about the volcanoes in Hawaii today? Cite evidence from the text in your response.

_____

_____

_____

Background When people hike and camp, they often leave behind trash such as bottles and wrappers. It's a big problem for the environment.

Setting a Purpose Read this play to find out how a group of kids make Earth a cleaner place.

Readers' Theater

The Big Cleanup

by Kate McGovern

1 Read As you read, look for text evidence.

- Circle the names of the characters listed in the Cast of Characters.
- Underline the words that tell where the play takes place.

Cast of Characters

Scott, leader of the "Clean Trails" team

Talia, a team member

Ricky, a team member

(A special team is preparing to clear garbage from Sunshine Point Park.)

2 Read As you read, look for text evidence.

- Circle the words Talia speaks in this part of the play.
- Underline the words that tell where the characters go.

Scott: Many people love to hike and camp in these hills. Some of them leave trash behind. We're going to help clean up! Does everyone have his or her equipment?

Talia: (holding up her trash bags) I do. These bags are for carrying down trash.

Ricky: These hiking boots will make it easier for us to climb the hills.

campsite:

(They arrive at a messy **campsite**.)

Scott: (looking around and frowning) Many hikers stopped here to rest as they **approached** the next hill. They left bottles, food containers, and even a tent!

approached:

3 Reread and Discuss Reread the page. What do readers learn about the cleanup from this part of the play? Cite text evidence in your discussion.

SHORT RESPONSE

Cite Text Evidence Stage directions appear in parentheses after two of the characters' names. How are these stage directions useful for readers? How are they useful for actors in a play? Cite details from the text in your response.

_____

_____

_____

_____

4 **Read** As you read, look for text evidence.

- Circle the stage directions in this part of the play.
- Underline a reason people should not leave trash in nature.

Ricky: People shouldn't treat the outdoors like a garbage dump! Nature is for everyone to enjoy.

Talia: Let's pick up this mess! When spring comes and the snow melts, we don't want trash to wash into the river.

onward:

Scott: (waving them **onward**) Let's go! This is the last section to climb.

5 **Reread** Reread the page. Why is it important for the kids to pick up the trash before spring? Cite text evidence in your response.

_____

_____

_____

6 Read As you read, look for text evidence.
Underline the words Ricky speaks in this part of the play.

Talia: This section is a lot trickier to climb in the winter. I'm glad the park ranger thought of adding this rope!

Scott: When we get to the top, we'll stop to rest. It's a clear day, so we should be able to see town from up there.

Ricky: I can't wait for a break. Let us remember to take our snack wrappers back down with us.

Scott: Yes! If we all do our part, Sunshine Point can stay clean for a long time.

7 Reread and Discuss Reread the page. Why do you think there are no stage directions in this part of the play? Cite text evidence in your discussion.

SHORT RESPONSE

Cite Text Evidence When Scott says, "If we all do our part," what is he talking about? Cite evidence in your response.

_____

_____

_____

_____

UNIT 6
Make Your Mark

Background Folktales are stories that have been told for a long time. They often tell how something in nature came to be. They may include a moral, or lesson, too.

Setting a Purpose Read the text to learn what happens when two animals have a race to win a big prize.

Paca and the Beetle

A FOLKTALE FROM BRAZIL

① Read As you read, look for text evidence.

- Circle the names of the three animals in the tale.
- Underline the sentence that tells what the winner of the race will get as a prize.

A beautiful red, blue, gold, and green macaw watched a brown beetle as it crawled across the jungle floor.

"Where are you going, my friend?" Macaw called out.

"I am going to the sea."

Just then, a paca skittered by.

"You?" Paca laughed. "You're so slow it will take you a hundred years!"

Macaw looked down. "You shouldn't brag, Paca. Why don't you race him? I'll give a new coat to whoever first reaches the big tree beside the river."

2 Read As you read, look for text evidence.

- Circle the words that tell about the photo.
- Underline a sentence that shows Paca is sure he will win the race, even before the race starts.

Paca laughed harder.

"This is no race!" he giggled. "You may as well give me the yellow coat and black spots of a **jaguar** right now!"

"I will race," Beetle said. "If I win, I would like a coat like yours, Macaw."

Paca **dashed** away. Then he thought, "Why should I hurry? I am so much faster than slow Beetle. I can take my time." He smiled, thinking of the fine new coat he would soon wear.

Scarlet macaws are found throughout South America. These spectacular birds are about three feet long from head to tail.

3 Reread and Discuss Reread the page and look at the photo. Why is it useful to see a photo of a scarlet macaw? How does it help you understand the story? Cite text evidence in your discussion.

SHORT RESPONSE

Cite Text Evidence Why does Paca decide to take his time after the start of the race? What does this tell you about him? Cite details from the text.

_____

_____

_____

_____

4 **Read** As you read, look for text evidence.

- Circle the words that tell the name of the beetle in the photo.
- Underline words that tell how Beetle is different from Paca.

When Paca neared the tree, however, he was amazed to see Beetle on a branch waiting for him.

Paca **gasped**. "How did you get here?" he **demanded**.

"I flew," Beetle answered with a smile.

"You have wings?" Paca asked.

Macaw answered. "Beetle doesn't brag about his wings, but he can use them when he needs to. Beetle is the winner."

gasped:

demanded:

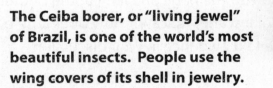

The Ceiba borer, or "living jewel" of Brazil, is one of the world's most beautiful insects. People use the wing covers of its shell in jewelry.

5 **Reread** Reread the page. Why is it important that Beetle didn't brag about his wings? Cite text evidence in your response.

_____

_____

_____

6 **Read** As you read, look for text evidence.

- Circle the words that tell where the spotted paca in the photo lives.
- Underline words that give a clue about Paca's mood at the end of the race.

Paca hung his head and slunk away, still wearing the brown coat with white spots he had always had. Then Macaw smiled at Beetle, and Beetle's hard back began to shine with the colors of Macaw's feathers. The beetle's shell has **gleamed** with a rainbow of colors ever since.

gleamed:

The spotted paca lives in the jungles of Brazil. It weighs between twelve and twenty-five pounds and is the world's second-largest rodent.

7 **Reread and Discuss** Reread the page. What happens when Macaw smiles at Beetle? Why? Cite text evidence in your discussion.

SHORT RESPONSE

(Cite Text Evidence) What do you think is the moral, or lesson, of this story? Cite text evidence in your response.

_____

_____

_____

_____

Background An electromagnet is a piece of metal that becomes magnetic when an electric current is passed through it. Electromagnets are in many items we use every day, as you'll find out in this text.

Setting a Purpose Read the text to learn about how electromagnets help you.

Electromagnets and You

① **Read** As you read, look for text evidence.
- Circle the title of this text.
- Underline the name of the device in the photo.

Ding-dong! Pressing a doorbell turns an electromagnet on. The magnet makes a striker or arm move. It hits a bell, and the doorbell rings.

② Read As you read, look for text evidence. Underline words that tell how an electromagnet makes a blow dryer work.

vacuum cleaner:

Did you know that electromagnets help you dry your hair? Any machine with an electric motor uses an electromagnet to turn working parts on and off. So a blow dryer, **vacuum cleaner**, refrigerator, washing machine, and radio all have electromagnets.

③ Reread and Discuss Reread the page. Why do you need electromagnets when you press the OFF button on a machine? Cite text evidence in your discussion.

SHORT RESPONSE

Cite Text Evidence How are all machines named on this page the same? Cite details from the text in your response.

_____

_____

_____

4 **Read** As you read, look for text evidence. Circle the word that names the machine in the photo.

Electromagnets even help you have fun! A computer uses electromagnets, too. Electromagnets help store information on the computer's **hard drive** so you can find it later.

hard drive:

5 **Reread** Reread the page and look back at the previous page. What do electromagnets do in computers that they don't do in blow dryers? Cite text evidence in your response.

_____

_____

_____

6 Read As you read, look for text evidence.

- Circle the name of the item shown in the photo.
- Underline words that tell what happens when electricity creates a magnetic field.

magnetic field:

Music pumps out of a stereo's speakers because of electromagnets. Inside, the cone has a coil attached to it. Around that is a magnet. Electricity creates a **magnetic field**. This vibrates, or shakes, the coil. The cone moves, too. That's what makes the sound you hear.

7 Reread and Discuss Reread the page. What parts inside a stereo speaker are needed to make sound? Cite text evidence in your discussion.

SHORT RESPONSE

Cite Text Evidence How would your life be different without electromagnets? Cite text evidence from this page and the rest of the text in your response.

_____

_____

_____

_____

_____

_____

Background Karate is a form of self-defense, or a way to protect yourself. It's also a sport. As you get better at karate, you earn belts of different colors. This text includes information about karate and a journal entry by someone who practices karate.

Setting a Purpose Read the text to find out what happens when a girl tries to win her blue belt in karate.

My Blue Belt Day!

CLOSE READ
Notes

1 **Read** As you read, look for text evidence.
Underline the words that tell what the word *karate* means.

ancient:

Karate is an **ancient** Asian form of self-defense. It uses no weapons. In fact, *karate* in Japanese means "empty hand." In karate, a person uses kicks, punches, blocks, and hand chops to stop an attacker.

2 Read As you read, look for text evidence.

- Circle the words that tell which students wear white belts in karate.
- Underline the words that tell how students get their next belt.

complicated:

master:

Belt colors show how much karate students have learned. Beginners wear white belts. A student must pass a test to achieve each next belt. The kicks and other moves get harder and more **complicated** with each level of belt. The highest level is the black belt, the sign of the **master**.

There are different schools of karate. Most follow this order of belts.

3 Reread and Discuss Reread the page. Why do students wear different belts in karate? Cite text evidence in your discussion.

SHORT RESPONSE

Cite Text Evidence What do students need to learn and do if they want to move to the next belt level? Cite details from the text in your response.

_____

_____

_____

_____

(4) **Read** As you read, look for text evidence.

- Circle the date when the journal entry was written.
- Underline colorful language the writer uses to describe how she felt before her karate test.

forms:

blocks:

roundhouse kick:

May 3

Why was I so scared this morning? My stomach was doing flips. You'd think I was facing a cougar instead of a karate test! I didn't feel scared six months ago. That's when I took my test to earn my green belt. I knew the green belt **forms** and performed all the kicks and **blocks** and punches just right. This morning, though, I didn't feel ready for the blue-belt test. I guess I was unsure about my **roundhouse kick**. The front kick, side kick, and roundhouse kick all need to be perfect to earn the blue belt.

(5) **Reread** Reread the page. How can you tell that this text is a journal entry? Cite text evidence in your response.

_____

_____

_____

6 **Read** As you read, look for text evidence. Underline words that tell what advice the girl's instructor gives her.

Just before my test, though, my instructor helped me. **Sensei** Scott said I just needed to focus. He said, "Don't think about earning your blue belt. Just think about each move as you do it."

It worked. I snapped my leg into a front kick. I whipped it out into a side kick. Then I shouted *"Yiah!"* and swung my right leg around for a perfect roundhouse kick.

Now I think that in six months I will be trading my blue belt for purple!

sensei:

7 **Reread and Discuss** Reread the page. What can you conclude about the writer's karate test based on the last sentence of her journal entry? Cite text evidence in your discussion.

SHORT RESPONSE

Cite Text Evidence What details and language does the writer use that help you understand what she is like and how she feels? Cite text evidence in your response.

_____

_____

_____

Background A spelling bee is a contest to find out who can spell best. No one knows for sure why it's called a *bee*. But the word *bee* has been used since the 1700s to describe a group of people getting together (sort of like bees in a hive).

Setting a Purpose Read the text to learn what it's like to take part in a big spelling contest.

C-H-A-M-P-I-O-N

① Read As you read, look for text evidence.
- Circle the name of the event this text is about.
- Underline the main idea of the third paragraph.

Imagine you are standing on a stage. Hundreds of people in the room are watching you. Millions are seeing you on TV. A man says, "The word is *champion*." It is up to you to spell it.

That's how kids in the national spelling bee feel.

Each year, more than 250 kids in elementary and middle school make it to the final bee. They come from all over the United States. A few even come from Canada, the Bahamas, and other countries.

2 Read As you read, look for text evidence.

- Circle the main idea of the first paragraph.
- Underline details that support that main idea.

Television helped make spelling bees popular. In 1994, the TV sports station ESPN started showing the national final bee. After that, spelling bees grew fast, and the bees got harder!

To get to the national bee, each speller works up through many smaller bees. A classroom bee might be the first one. The winner then **competes** against students from other classrooms in the school. One student will win. That winner will spell against students from other local schools. Finally, the Scripps National Spelling Bee is held in Washington, D.C., and shown on TV.

competes:

3 Reread and Discuss Reread the page. What is the main idea of the second paragraph? What details support it? Cite text evidence in your discussion.

SHORT RESPONSE

(Cite Text Evidence) What can you conclude about why television helped make spelling bees popular? Cite details from the text in your response.

_____

_____

_____

_____

④ **Read** As you read, look for text evidence.

- Circle the main idea of each paragraph.
- Underline a sentence that explains how students correctly spell words they haven't heard before.

pressure:

fainted:

Getting to the finals is hard work. The ones who make it study and practice day after day. They learn base words and roots. That helps them correctly spell words that they have never even heard before.

The spellers face a lot of **pressure**. To win, they have to spell harder and harder words. One year, a speller **fainted** at the microphone. Before anyone could help him, he jumped up and correctly spelled his word!

⑤ **Reread** Reread the page. Why do the spellers face more pressure as they try to make it to the finals? Cite text evidence in your response.

_____

_____

_____

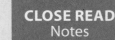

6 Read As you read, look for text evidence

- Circle the words that tell about the photo.
- Underline a detail that explains why Katharine Close seemed "cool" on TV.

admitted:

charm:

    Another year, Katharine Close won by correctly spelling *ursprache*. Most adults don't even know what that word means. (It means "an early language.") Katharine seemed very cool on TV. She just stood with her hands in her pockets and spelled word after word.

    Later, Katharine **admitted** she was not as cool as she looked. Her hand was in her pocket to hold her good-luck **charm**. It worked!

2006: When 13-year-old Katharine Close won the national spelling bee in 2006, it was her fifth time in the finals.

7 Reread and Discuss Reread the page. Why does the author say that Katharine's good-luck charm worked? Do you think the author really believes this? Cite text evidence in your discussion.

SHORT RESPONSE

Cite Text Evidence What details can you learn from the caption that you can't learn from the main text? What do these details help you understand about Katharine Close? Cite evidence from the text in your response.

_____

_____

_____

Background This news article is about a theater in Evanston, Illinois. You'll see this place name listed at the beginning of the article. Many news articles start with the name of the place where the story happens.

Setting a Purpose Read the text to learn about a special theater that brings together people of all ages.

Acting Across Generations

① Read As you read, look for text evidence.

- Circle the words that tell where this article takes place.
- Underline the name of the play that the theater put on.

EVANSTON, ILLINOIS When the Evanston Children's Theatre decided to put on a play of *Charlotte's Web*, they invited kids from eight to twelve years old to try out for parts. They asked seniors age 55 and older to try out, too. Usually, child actors wear gray wigs and paste on fake beards and moustaches to look old. This group uses real seniors.

2 Read As you read, look for text evidence.

- Circle a fact about when the children's theater began in the Levy Center.
- Underline the words that tell why kids play most parts in the theater.

A few years ago, the Evanston city council decided that the children's theater would have its home in the Levy Center, Evanston's new senior center. So it just seemed natural to get both the kids and the seniors working together.

This experiment has worked well for several plays. Kids play most parts. It's a children's theater group, after all. But seniors have one or two **roles** in each play.

roles:

The Evanston Children's Theatre has become very popular. In fact, more than 300 people came to a Sunday afternoon performance of *Charlotte's Web*.

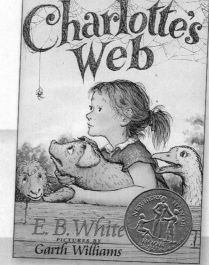

3 Reread and Discuss Reread the page. Why did it make sense to have kids and seniors work together in the theater? Cite text evidence in your discussion.

SHORT RESPONSE

Cite Text Evidence What fact can you learn from the photo caption that you can't learn from the main text? Cite details from the text in your response.

_____

_____

_____

4 Read As you read, look for text evidence.

- Circle the words that tell about the photo.
- Underline words in the main text that tell which seniors might take part in the children's theater.

try out:

The Levy Center holds different senior classes. Seniors who take acting classes **try out** for the children's theater. Working with kids keeps seniors young. Working with seniors helps kids, too. The seniors share tips from their acting classes, and the kids show what they've learned.

Seniors and children act in a play together.

5 Reread Reread the page. How do the seniors' acting classes help both seniors and kids at the theater? Cite text evidence in your response.

_____

_____

_____

6 **Read** As you read, look for text evidence.
Underline a sentence that tells a way actors help one another.

lines:

To put on a play, actors must help one another. If a
senior forgets some **lines**, kids jump right in and move
the **scene** along. Seniors do the same for the kids. Once
a senior got sick after the first show. A kid took on the
senior's part. The show must go on—and it did!

scene:

Putting on plays is great fun, but the
Evanston Children's Theatre gives
seniors and kids a chance to help
one another. **Bravo!**

bravo:

7 **Reread and Discuss** Reread the page.
What do you think "the show must go on" means? What details help you
understand the meaning of this phrase? Cite text evidence in your discussion.

SHORT RESPONSE

Cite Text Evidence What are the most important facts readers can learn
from this news story? Cite evidence from this page and the rest of the
text in your response.

_____

_____

_____

Acknowledgments

"A Bat is Born" from *The Bat-Poet* by Randall Jarrell. Text copyright © 1964 by Randall Jarrell. Reprinted by permission of The Estate of Randall Jarrell.

Excerpt from *Charlotte's Web* by E.B. White, illustrated by Garth Williams. Text copyright 1952, renewed © 1980 by E.B. White. Illustrations copyright 1952, renewed © 1980 by Garth Williams. Reprinted by permission of HarperCollins Publishers.

Excerpt from "My Smelly Pet" from *Judy Moody* by Megan McDonald, illustrated by Peter H. Reynolds. Text copyright © 2000 by Megan McDonald. Illustrations copyright © 2000 by Peter H. Reynolds. Reprinted by permission of the publisher, Candlewick Press, Somerville, MA, Megan McDonald and Santillana Ediciones Generales, Spain.

"Stopping by Woods on a Snowy Evening" from *The Poetry of Robert Frost* by Robert Frost, edited by Edward Connery Lathem. Text copyright © 1923, 1969 by Henry Holt and Company, text copyright © 1951 by Robert Frost. Reprinted by permission of Henry Holt and Company, LLC.